XIAOJING

The Classic of Filial Piety

CONFUCIUS

Translated by
JAMES LEGGE

CONTENTS

The Scope and Meaning of the Treatise 開宗明義	1
Filial Piety in the Son of Heaven 天子	4
Filial Piety in the Princes of States 諸侯	6
Filial Piety in High Ministers and Great Officers 卿大夫	9
Filial Piety in Inferior Officers 士	12
Filial Piety in the Common People 庶人	15
Filial Piety in Relation to the Three Powers (Heaven, Earth, Man) 三才	17
Filial Piety in Government 孝治	20

The Government of the Sages (the sovereigns of antiquity) 聖治	23
An Orderly Description of the Acts of Filial Piety 紀孝行	29
Filial Piety in Relation to the Five Punishments 五刑	31
Amplification of "The All-embracing Rule of Conduct" in Chapter I 廣要道	33
Amplification of 'the Perfect Virtue' in Chapter I 廣至德	35
Amplification of "Making our Name Famous" in Chapter I 廣揚名	37
Filial Piety in Relation to Reproof and Remonstrance 諫諍	39
The Influence of Filial Piety and the Response to It 感應	42
The Service of the Ruler 事君	45
Filial Piety in Mourning for Parents 喪親	47

THE SCOPE AND MEANING OF THE TREATISE
開宗明義

仲尼居，曾子侍。子曰：「先王有至德要道，以順天下，民用和睦，上下無怨。汝知之乎？」曾子避席曰：「參不敏，何足以知之？」子曰：「夫孝，德之本也，教之所由生也。復坐，吾語汝。身體髮膚，受之父母，不敢毀傷，孝之始也。立身行道，揚名於後世，以顯父母，孝之終也。夫孝，始於事親，中於事君，終於立身。《大雅》云：『無念爾祖，聿脩厥德。』」

(Once), when Zhong Ni[1] was unoccupied, and his disciple Zeng[2] was sitting by in attendance on him, the Master said, "The ancient kings had a perfect virtue and all-embracing rule of conduct, through which they were in accord with all under heaven. By the practice of it the people were brought to live in peace and harmony, and there was no ill-will between superiors and inferiors. Do you know what it was?"

Zeng rose from his mat and said, "How should I, Shen, who am so devoid of intelligence, be able to know this?"

The Master said, "(It was filial piety.) Now filial piety is the root of (all) virtue,[3] and (the stem) out of which grows (all moral) teaching. Sit down again, and I will explain the subject to you. Our bodies—to every hair and bit of skin—are received by us from our parents, and we must not presume to injure or wound them. This is the beginning of filial piety. When we have established our character by the practice of the (filial) course, so as to make our name famous in future ages and thereby glorify our parents, this is the end of filial piety. It commences with the service of parents; it proceeds to the service of the ruler; it is completed by the establishment of character.

"It is said in the Major Odes of the Kingdom:

> *Ever think of your ancestor,*
> *Cultivating your virtue.*"[4]

---

1. This is the zi or "style" of Confucius.
2. Zeng Zi speaks in fourteen sayings in the *Analects*, e.g., 1.4. He names himself a bit later by his ming or "given name," Shen. His name is traditionally associated with the virtue of filial piety; see, for example, *Analects* 1.9 & 19.17 & 18.
3. "All virtue" means the five virtuous principles, the constituents of humanity: benevolence, righteousness, propriety, knowledge, and fidelity.
4. Shi III, i, ode 1, stanza 6, p. 431. Mao 235.

FILIAL PIETY IN THE SON OF HEAVEN
天子

子曰：「愛親者，不敢惡於人；敬親者，不敢慢於人。愛敬盡於事親，而德教加於百姓，刑於四海。蓋天子之孝也。《甫刑》云：『一人有慶，兆民賴之。』」

The Master said, "He who loves his parents will not dare (to incur the risk of) being hated by any man, and he who reveres his parents will not dare (to incur the risk of) being contemned by any man.[1] When the love and reverence (of the Son of Heaven) are thus carried to the utmost in the service of his parents, the lessons of his virtue affect all the people, and he becomes a pattern to (all within) the four seas. This is the filial piety of the Son of Heaven.

"It is said in (the Marquis of) Fu on Punishments:

> *The One man will have felicity,*
> *and the millions of the people will*
>   *depend on (what ensures his*
>   *happiness)."*[2]

---

1. Many translators have missed the passive force of this construction.
2. Shu Jing, vol III of *The Chinese Classics*, p. 600.

FILIAL PIETY IN THE PRINCES OF STATES
諸侯

在上不驕，高而不危；制節謹度，滿而不溢。高而不危，所以長守貴也。滿而不溢，所以長守富也。富貴不離其身，然後能保其社稷，而和其民人。蓋諸侯之孝也。《詩》云：「戰戰兢兢，如臨深淵，如履薄冰。」

"Above others, and yet free from pride, they dwell on high, without peril. Adhering to economy and carefully observant of the rules and laws, they are full, without overflowing. To dwell on high without peril is the way long to preserve nobility; to be full without overflowing is the way long to preserve riches. When their riches and nobility do not leave their persons, then they are able to preserve the altars of their land and grain, and to secure the harmony of their people and men in office.[1] This is the filial piety of the princes of states.

"It is said in the Book of Poetry:

> *Be apprehensive, be cautious,*
> *As if on the brink of a deep abyss,*
> *As if treading on thin ice.*"[2]

---

1. The king had a great altar to the spirit (or spirits) presiding over the land. The color of the earth in the center of it was yellow; that on each of its four sides differed according to the colors assigned to the four quarters of the sky. A portion of this earth was cut away and formed the nucleus of a corresponding altar in each feudal state, according to their position relative to the capital. The prince of the state had the prerogative of sacrificing there. A similar rule prevailed for the altars to the spirits presiding over the grain. So long as a family ruled in a state, so long

its chief offered those sacrifices; and the extinction of the sacrifices was an emphatic way of describing the ruin and extinction of the ruling house.
2. Shi, II, v, ode 1, stanza 6, p. 333. Mao 195. This passage is cited by Zeng Zi in *Analects* 8.3.

FILIAL PIETY IN HIGH MINISTERS AND GREAT OFFICERS

卿大夫

非先王之法服不敢服，非先王之法言不敢道，非先王之德行不敢行。是故非法不言，非道不行；口無擇言，身無擇行。言滿天下無口過，行滿天下無怨惡。三者備矣，然後能守其宗廟。蓋卿、大夫之孝也。《詩》云：「夙夜匪懈，以事一人。」

"They do not presume to wear robes other than those appointed by the laws of the ancient kings, nor to speak words other than those sanctioned by their speech, nor to exhibit conduct other than that exemplified by their virtuous ways. Thus none of their words being contrary to those sanctions, and none of their actions contrary to the (right) way, from their mouths there comes no exceptionable speech, and in their conduct there are found no exceptionable actions. Their words may fill all under heaven, and no error of speech will be found in them. Their actions may fill all under heaven, and no dissatisfaction or dislike will be awakened by them. When these three things—(their robes, their words, and their conduct)—are all complete as they should be, they can then preserve their ancestral temples.[1] This is the filial piety of high ministers and great officers.

"It is said in the Book of Poetry:

He is never idle, day or night,
In the service of the One man."[2]

---

1. Their ancestral temples were to the ministers and grand officers what the altars of their land and

grain were to the feudal lords. Every great officer had three temples or shrines, in which he sacrificed to the first chief of his family or clan, to his grandfather, and to his father. While these remained, the family remained, and its honors were prepetuated.
2. Shi, III, iii, ode 6, stanza 4, p. 543. Mao 260.

FILIAL PIETY IN INFERIOR OFFICERS

士

資於事父以事母，而愛同；資於事父以事君，而敬同。故母取其愛，而君取其敬，兼之者父也。故以孝事君則忠，以敬事長則順。忠順不失，以事其上，然後能保其祿位，而守其祭祀。蓋士之孝也。《詩》云：「夙興夜寐，無忝爾所生」。

"As they serve their fathers, so they serve their mothers, and they love them equally. As they serve their fathers, so they serve their rulers, and they reverence them equally. Hence love is what is chiefly rendered to the mother, and reverence is what is chiefly rendered to the ruler, while both of these things are given to the father. Therefore when they serve their ruler with filial piety, they are loyal; when they serve their superiors with reverence, they are obedient. Not failing in this loyalty and obedience in serving those above them, they are then able to preserve their emoluments and positions, and to maintain their sacrifices.[1] This is the filial piety of inferior officers.[2]

"It is said in the Book of Poetry:

> *Rising early and going to sleep*
> *late,*
> *Do not disgrace those who gave*
> *you birth."*[3]

---

1. These officers had their 'positions' or places, and their pay. They had also their sacrifices, but such as were private or personal to themselves.
2. not 'scholar,' a more modern meaning of shi. The shi of feudal China were the younger sons of the

higher classes, and men that by their ability were rising out of the lower, and who were all in inferior situations and looking forward to offices of trust in the service of the royal court or of their several states. When the feudal system had passed away, the class of 'scholars' gradually took their place.
3. Shi, II, v, ode 2, stanza 4, p. 335. Mao 196.

FILIAL PIETY IN THE COMMON PEOPLE

庶人

用天之道，分地之利，謹身節用，以養父母，此庶人之孝也。故自天子至於庶人，孝無終始，而患不及者，未之有也。

"They follow the course of heaven (in the revolving seasons); they distinguish the advantages afforded by (different) soils; they are careful of their conduct and economical in their expenditure—in order to nourish their parents. This is the filial piety of the common people.

"Therefore from the Son of Heaven down

to the common people, there never has been one whose filial piety was without its beginning and end on whom calamity did not come."[1]

---

1. This chapter is the end of what Zhu Xi regarded as the only portion of the Xiao that came directly from Confucius. The chapters that follow lack the sequence of the foregoing.

FILIAL PIETY IN RELATION TO THE THREE POWERS (HEAVEN, EARTH, MAN)

三才

曾子曰：「甚哉，孝之大也！」子曰：「夫孝，天之經也，地之義也，民之行也。天地之經，而民是則之。則天之明，因地之利，以順天下。是以其教不肅而成，其政不嚴而治。先王見教之可以化民也，是故先之以博愛，而民莫遺其親，陳之德義，而民興行。先之以敬讓，而民不爭；導之以禮樂，而民和睦；示之以好惡，而民知禁。《詩》云：『赫赫師尹，民具爾瞻。』」

The disciple Zeng said, "Immense indeed is the greatness of filial piety!"

The Master replied,[1] "Yes, filial piety is the constant (method) of Heaven, the righteousness of Earth, and the practical duty of Man. Heaven and earth invariably pursue the course (that may be thus described), and the people take it as their pattern. (The ancient kings) imitated the brilliant luminaries of heaven and acted in accordance with the (varying) advantages afforded by earth, so that they were in accord with all under heaven, and in consequence their teachings, without being severe, were successful, and their government, without being rigorous, secured perfect order.

"The ancient kings, seeing how their teachings could transform the people, set before them therefore an example of the most extended love, and none of the people neglected their parents. They set forth to them (the nature of) virtue and righteousness, and the people roused themselves to the practice of them. They went before them with reverence and yielding courtesy, and the people had no contentions. They led them on by the rules of propriety and by music, and the people were harmonious and benignant. They showed them what they loved and what they disliked, and the people understood their prohibitions.

"It is said in the Book of Poetry:

Awe-inspiring are you, O
Grand-Master Yin,
And the people all look up to
you."[2]

---

1. The first part of Confucius' reply is found in the *Zuo Zhuan* (Legge, vol. V, p. 708)
2. Shi, II, iv, ode 7, stanza 1, p. 309. Mao 191.

FILIAL PIETY IN GOVERNMENT
孝治

子曰：「昔者明王之以孝治天下也，不敢遺小國之臣，而況於公、侯、伯、子、男乎？故得萬國之歡心，以事其先王。治國者，不敢侮於鰥寡，而況於士民乎？故得百姓之歡心，以事其先君。治家者，不敢失於臣妾，而況於妻子乎？故得人之歡心，以事其親。夫然，故生則親安之，祭則鬼享之。是以天下和平，災害不生，禍亂不作。故明王之以孝治天下也如此。《詩》云：『有覺德行，四國順之。』」

The Master said, "Anciently, when the intelligent kings by means of filial piety ruled all under heaven, they did not dare to receive with disrespect the ministers of small states. How much less would they do so to the dukes, marquises, counts, and barons! Thus it was that they got (the princes of) the myriad states with joyful hearts (to assist them) in the (sacrificial) services to their royal predecessors.

"The rulers of states did not dare to slight wifeless men and widows. How much less would they slight their officers and the people! Thus it was that they got all their people with joyful hearts (to assist them) in serving the rulers, their predecessors.

"The heads of clans did not dare to slight their servants and concubines. How much less would they slight their wives and sons! Thus it was that they got their men with joyful hearts (to assist them) in the service of their parents.

"In such a state of things, while alive, parents reposed in (the glory of) their sons, and, when sacrificed to, their disembodied spirits enjoyed their offerings. Therefore for all under heaven peace and harmony prevailed; disasters and calamities did not occur; misfortunes and rebellions did not arise.

"It is said in the Book of Poetry:

To an upright, virtuous conduct
All in the four quarters of the state
render obedient homage."[1]

---

1. Shi Jing, III, iii, ode 2, stanza 2, p. 511. Mao 256.

THE GOVERNMENT OF THE SAGES (THE SOVEREIGNS OF ANTIQUITY)

聖治

曾子曰：「敢問聖人之德，無以加於孝乎？」子曰：「天地之性，人爲貴。人之行，莫大於孝。孝莫大於嚴父。嚴父莫大於配天，則周公其人也。昔者，周公郊祀後稷以配天，宗祀文王於明堂，以配上帝。是以四海之內，各以其職來祭。夫聖人之德，又何以加於孝乎？故親生之膝下，以養父母日嚴。聖人因嚴以教敬，因親以教愛。聖人之教，不肅而成，其政不嚴而治，其所因者本也。父子之道，天性也，君臣之義也。父母生之，續莫大焉。君親臨之，厚莫重焉。故不愛其親而愛他人者，謂之悖德；不敬其親而敬他人者，謂之悖禮。以順則逆，民無則焉。不在於善，而皆在於凶德，雖得之，君子不貴也。君子則不然，言思可道，行思可樂，德義可尊，作事可法，容止可觀，進退可度，以臨其民。是以其民畏而愛之，則而象之。故能成其德教，而行其政令。《詩》云：『淑人君子，其儀不忒。』」

The disciple Zeng said, "I venture to ask whether in the virtue of the sages there was not something greater than filial piety."

The Master replied, "Of all (creatures with their different) natures produced by Heaven and Earth, man is the noblest. Of all the actions of man there is none greater than filial piety. In

filial piety there is nothing greater than the reverential awe of one's father. In the reverential awe shown to one's father there is nothing greater than the making him the correlate of Heaven.[1] The duke of Zhou was the man who (first) did this.

"Formerly the duke of Zhou at the border

altar sacrificed to Hou Ji as the correlate of Heaven, and in the Brilliant Hall he honored king Wen and sacrificed to him as the correlate of God. The consequence was that from (all the states) within the four seas, every (prince) came in the discharge of his duty to (assist in those) sacrifices. In the virtue of the sages what besides was there greater than filial piety?

"Now the feeling of affection grows up at the parents' knees, and as (the duty of) nourishing those parents is exercised, the affection daily merges in awe. The sages proceeded from the (feeling of) awe to teach (the duties of) reverence, and from (that of) affection to teach (those of) love. The teachings of the sages, without being severe, were successful, and their government, without being rigorous, was effective. What they proceeded from was the root (of filial piety implanted by Heaven).

"The relation and duties between father and son, (thus belonging to) the Heaven-conferred nature, (contain in them the principle of) righteousness between ruler and subject. The son derives his life from his parents, and no greater gift could possibly be transmitted. His ruler and parent (in one), his father deals with him accordingly, and no generosity could be greater than this. Hence, he who does not love his parents, but loves other men, is called a rebel against virtue, and he who does not revere his parents, but reveres other men, is called a rebel against propriety. When (the ruler) himself thus acts contrary to (the principles) which should place him in accord (with all men), he presents nothing for the people to imitate. He has nothing to do with what is good, but entirely and only with what is injurious to virtue. Though he may get (his will, and be above others), the superior man does not give him his approval.

"It is not so with the superior man. He speaks, having thought whether the words should be spoken; he acts, having thought whether his actions are sure to give pleasure. His virtue and righteousness are such as will be honored; what he initiates and does is fit to be imitated; his deportment is worthy of contemplation; his movements in advancing or retiring are all according to the proper rule. In this way does he present himself to the people, who both revere and love him, imitate and become like him. Thus he is able to make his teaching of virtue successful, and his government and orders to be carried into effect.[2]

"It is said in the Book of Poetry:

*The virtuous man, the princely
  one,
Has nothing wrong in his
  deportment.*"[3]

---

1. pei tian. The phrase is used with reference to the virtue of a sovereign, making him as it were the mate of God, ruling on earth as God rules above, and with reference to the honors paid to a departed sovereign, when he is associated with God in the great sacrificial services. In the next para-

graph, 'correlate of God' renders pei shang di. Legge has a long discussion of his rendering of the terms tian and shang di in his preface, pp. xxiii-xxix. In addition, in his note, Legge explains that "Heaven" and "God" have the same reference; the former expresses honor, the latter affection.
2. This paragraph is a mosaic of passages from the *Zuo Zhuan*.
3. Shi, I, xiv, ode 3, stanza 3, p. 223. Mao 152.

AN ORDERLY DESCRIPTION OF THE ACTS OF FILIAL PIETY

紀孝行

子曰：「孝子之事親也，居則致其敬，養則致其樂，病則致其憂，喪則致其哀，祭則致其嚴。五者備矣，然後能事親。事親者，居上不驕，爲下不亂，在醜不爭。居上而驕則亡，爲下而亂則刑，在醜而爭則兵。三者不除，雖日用三牲之養，猶爲不孝也。」

The Master said, "The service which a filial son does to his parents is as follows: In his general conduct to them, he manifests the utmost reverence. In his nourishing of them, his endeavor is to give them the utmost pleasure. When they are ill, he feels the greatest anxiety. In mourning for them (dead), he exhibits every demonstration of grief. In sacrificing to them, he displays the utmost solemnity. When a son is complete in these five things, (he may be pronounced) able to serve his parents.

"He who (thus) serves his parents, in a high situation will be free from pride, in a low situation will be free from insubordination, and among his equals will not be quarrelsome. In a high situation pride leads to ruin; in a low situation insubordination leads to punishment; among equals quarrelsomeness leads to the wielding of weapons. If those three things be not put away, though a son every day contribute beef, mutton, and pork to nourish his parents, he is not filial."[1]

---

1. Cf. *Analects* 2.7.

FILIAL PIETY IN RELATION TO THE FIVE PUNISHMENTS

五刑

子曰：「五刑之屬三千，而罪莫大於不孝。要君者無上，非聖人者無法，非孝者無親。此大亂之道也。」

The Master said, "There are three thousand offenses against which the five punishments are directed,[1] and there is not one of them greater than being unfilial.

"When constraint is put upon a ruler, that is the disowning of his superiority. When the authority of the sages is disallowed, that is the disowning of (all) law. When filial piety is put aside, that is the disowning of the principle of affection. These (three things) pave the way to anarchy."

---

1. Cf. Shu, Legge, vol. III, p. 44-45 and esp. p. 388-390.

AMPLIFICATION OF "THE ALL-EMBRACING RULE OF CONDUCT" IN CHAPTER I

廣要道

子曰：「教民親愛，莫善於孝。教民禮順，莫善於悌。移風易俗，莫善於樂。安上治民，莫善於禮。禮者，敬而已矣。故敬其父，則子悅；敬其兄，則弟悅；敬其君，則臣悅；敬一人，而千萬人悅。所敬者寡，而悅者眾，此之謂要道也。」

The Master said, "For teaching the people to be affectionate and loving, there is nothing better than filial piety. For teaching them (the observance of) propriety and submissiveness, there is nothing better than fraternal duty. For changing their manners and altering their customs, there is nothing better than music. For securing the repose of superiors and the good order of the people, there is nothing better than the rules of propriety.

"The rules of propriety are simply (the development of) the principle of reverence. Therefore the reverence paid to a father makes (all) sons pleased. The reverence paid to an elder brother makes (all) younger brothers pleased. The reverence paid to a ruler makes (all) subjects pleased. The reverence paid to the One man makes thousands and myriads of men pleased. The reverence is paid to a few, and the pleasure extends to many. This is what is meant by an 'All-embracing Rule of Conduct.'"

AMPLIFICATION OF 'THE PERFECT VIRTUE' IN CHAPTER I

廣至德

子曰：「君子之教以孝也，非家至而日見之也。教以孝，所以敬天下之爲人父者也。教以悌，所以敬天下之爲人兄者也。教以臣，所以敬天下之爲人君者也。《詩》云：『愷悌君子，民之父母。』非至德，其孰能順民如此其大者乎！」

The Master said, "The teaching of filial piety by the superior man[1] does not require that he should go to family after family and daily see the members of each. His teaching of filial piety is a tribute of reverence to all the fathers under heaven. His teaching of fraternal submission is a tribute of reverence to all the elder brothers under heaven. His teaching of the duty of a subject is a tribute of reverence to all the rulers under heaven.

"It is said in the Book of Poetry:

> *The happy and courteous sovereign*
> *Is the parent of the people.*[2]

"If it were not a perfect virtue, how could it be recognized as in accordance with their nature by the people so extensively as this?"

---

1. The jun zi here must be taken to mean the sovereign.
2. Shi, III, ii, ode 7, stanza 1, p. 489. Mao 251.

AMPLIFICATION OF "MAKING OUR NAME FAMOUS" IN CHAPTER I

廣揚名

子曰：「君子之事親孝，故忠可移於君。事兄悌，故順可移於長。居家理，故治可移於官。是以行成於內，而名立於後世矣。」

The Master said, "The filial piety with which the superior man serves his parents may be transferred as loyalty to the ruler. The fraternal duty with which he serves his elder brother may be transferred as submissive deference to elders. His regulation of his family may be transferred as good government in any official position. Therefore, when his conduct is thus successful in his inner (private) circle, his name will be established (and transmitted) to future generations."

FILIAL PIETY IN RELATION TO REPROOF AND REMONSTRANCE

諫諍

曾子曰：「若夫慈愛、恭敬、安親、揚名，則聞命矣。敢問子從父之令，可謂孝乎？」子曰：「是何言與，是何言與！昔者天子有爭臣七人，雖無道，不失其天下；諸侯有爭臣五人，雖無道，不失其國；大夫有爭臣三人，雖無道，不失其家；士有爭友，則身不離於令名；父有爭子，則身不陷於不義。故當不義，則子不可以不爭於父，臣不可以不爭於君；故當不義，則爭之。從父之令，又焉得爲孝乎！」

The disciple Zeng said, "I have heard your instructions on the affection of love, on respect and reverence, on giving repose to (the minds of) our parents, and on making our names famous. I would venture to ask if (simple) obedience to the orders of one's father can be pronounced filial piety."

The Master replied, "What words are these! What words are these! Anciently, if the Son of Heaven had seven ministers who would remonstrate with him, although he had not right methods of government, he would not lose his possession of the kingdom. If the prince of a state had five such ministers, though his measures might be equally wrong, he would not lose his state. If a great officer had three, he would not, in a similar case, lose (the headship of) his clan. If an inferior officer had a friend who would remonstrate with him, a good name would not cease to be connected with his character. And the father who had a son that would remonstrate with him would not sink into the gulf of unrighteous deeds. Therefore when a case of unrighteous conduct is concerned, a son must by no means keep from remonstrating with his father, nor a minister from remonstrating with his ruler. Hence, since remonstrance is required in the case of unrighteous conduct, how can (simple) obedience to the orders of a father be accounted filial piety?"[1]

---

1. Cf. *Analects* 4.18 and Li Ji, X, i, 15.

THE INFLUENCE OF FILIAL PIETY AND THE RESPONSE TO IT

感應

子曰：「昔者明王事父孝，故事天明；事母孝，故事地察；長幼順，故上下治。天地明察，神明彰矣。故雖天子，必有尊也，言有父也；必有先也，言有兄也。宗廟致敬，不忘親也；修身慎行，恐辱先也。宗廟致敬，鬼神著矣。孝悌之至，通於神明，光於四海，無所不通。《詩》云：『自西自東，自南自北，無思不服。』」

The Master said, "Anciently, the intelligent kings served their fathers with filial piety, and therefore they served Heaven with intelligence. They served their mothers with filial piety, and therefore they served Earth with discrimination. They pursued the right course with reference to their (own) seniors and juniors, and therefore they secured the regulation of the relations between superiors and inferiors (throughout the kingdom). When Heaven and Earth were served with intelligence and discrimination, the spiritual intelligences displayed (their retributive power).[1]

"Therefore even the Son of Heaven must have some whom he honors; that is, he has his uncles of his surname. He must have some to whom he concedes the precedence; that is, he has his cousins, who bear the same surname and are older than himself. In the ancestral temple he manifests the utmost reverence, showing that he does not forget his parents. He cultivates his person and is careful of his conduct, fearing lest he should disgrace his predecessors. When in the ancestral temple he exhibits the utmost reverence, the spirits of the departed manifest themselves. Perfect filial piety and fraternal duty reach to (and move) the spiritual intelligences and diffuse their light on all within the four seas. They penetrate everywhere.

"It is said in the Book of Poetry:

> *From the west to the east,*
> *From the south to the north,*
> *There was not a thought but did*
> *him homage."*[2]

---

1. The "spiritual intelligences" here are Heaven and Earth conceived of as spiritual beings.
2. Shi, III, i, ode 10, stanza 6, p. 463. Mao 244.

THE SERVICE OF THE RULER

事君

子曰：「君子之事上也，進思盡忠，退思補過，將順其美，匡救其惡，故上下能相親也。《詩》云：『心乎愛矣，遐不謂矣，中心藏之，何日忘之。』」

The Master said, "The superior man[1] serves his ruler in such a way that, when at court in his presence, his thought is how to discharge his loyal duty to the utmost, and when he retires from it, his thought is how to amend his errors. He carries out with deference the measures springing from his excellent qualities and rectifies him (only) to save him from what are evil. Hence, as the superior and inferior, they are able to have an affection for each other.

"It is said in the Book of Poetry:

In my heart I love him,
And why should I not say so?
In the core of my heart I keep him,
And never will forget him."[2]

---

1. Jun zi here can only be the good and intelligent officer in the royal domain or at a feudal court.
2. Shi, II, viii, ode 4, stanza 4, p. 415. Mao 228.

FILIAL PIETY IN MOURNING FOR PARENTS
喪親

子曰：「孝子之喪親也，哭不偯，禮無容，言不文，服美不安，聞樂不樂，食旨不甘，此哀慼之情也。三日而食，教民無以死傷生。毀不滅性，此聖人之政也。喪不過三年，示民有終也。爲之棺槨衣衾而舉之，陳其簠簋而哀慼之；擗踴哭泣，哀以送之；卜其宅兆，而安措之；爲之宗廟，以鬼享之；春秋祭祀，以時思之。生事愛敬，死事哀慼，生民之本盡矣，死生之義備矣，孝子之事親終矣。」

The Master said, "When a filial son is mourning for a parent, he wails, but not with a prolonged sobbing. In the movements of ceremony he pays no attention to his appearance. His words are without elegance of phrase. He cannot bear to wear fine clothes. When he hears music, he feels no delight. When he eats a delicacy, he is not conscious of its flavor. Such is the nature of grief and sorrow.

"After three days he may partake of food, for thus the people are taught that the living should not be injured on account of the dead, and that emaciation must not be carried to the extinction of life. Such is the rule of the sages. The period of mourning does not go beyond three years, to show the people that it must have an end.

"An inner and outer coffin are made; the grave-clothes also are put on, and the shroud; and (the body) is lifted (into the coffin). The sacrificial vessels, round and square, are (regularly) set forth, and (the sight of them) fills (the mourners) with (fresh) distress. The women beat their breasts, and the men stamp with their feet, wailing and weeping, while they sorrowfully escort the coffin to the grave. They consult the tortoise-shell to determine the grave and the ground about it, and there they lay the body in peace. They prepare the ancestral temple (to receive the tablet of the departed), and there they present offerings to the disembodied spirit. In spring and autumn they offer sacrifices, thinking of the deceased as the seasons come round.

"The services of love and reverence to parents when alive, and those of grief and sorrow to them when dead: these completely discharge the fundamental duty of living men. The righteous claims of life and death are all satisfied, and the filial son's service of his parents is completed."[1]

---

1. The above is the *Classic of Filial Piety*, as published by the emperor Xuan in A.D. 722, with the head-

ings then prefixed to the eighteen chapters. Subsequently, in the eleventh century, Si Ma Guang (A.D. 1009-1086), a famous statesman and historian, published what he thought was the more ancient text of the classic in twenty-two chapters, with "Explanations" by himself, without chapter numbering or headings. The differences between his text and that of the Tang emperor are insignificant.

Copyright © 2020 by FV Éditions
Cover Design : FVE
Ebook ISBN : 979-10-299-1037-1
Paperback ISBN : 979-10-299-1038-8
Hardcover ISBN : 979-10-299-1039-5
All rights reserved.

Also Available

THE GREAT LEARNING

www.ingramcontent.com/pod-product-compliance
Lightning Source LLC
LaVergne TN
LVHW041556070526
838199LV00046B/1992